NORTH EAST of SCOTLAND LIBRARY SERVICE
MELDRUM MEG WAY, OLDMELDRUM

KIDD, TED

Tell it to an
Aberdonian! humour of
the North-East

X6

239098

HUMOUR OF THE NORTH-EAST

Tell it to an Aberdonian!

By TED KIDD

Drawings by Rod

$$\frac{x6}{21}$$

239098

"TELL IT TO AN ABERDONIAN! — WIT AND HUMOUR OF SCOTLAND'S NORTH EAST" was published in 1989 by Lang Syne Publishers Ltd, Old School, Blanefield, Glasgow G63 9HX and printed by Waterside Printers at the same address.
ISBN: 185217 1464

ABOUT THE AUTHOR.

TED KIDD is one of the North-East's best known and best loved newspapermen. For many years he was Bureau Chief of the Daily Record's Aberdeen office and covered the big local news stories that made headlines around the world. Now he is enjoying life at a less hectic pace which is great news for us all — because he found the time to put together this superb booklet full of entertaining snippets gleamed from long hours at the bar of the "university of life."

INTRODUCTION

THE NORTH-EAST of Scotland sticks out like a knuckle from the rest of the Scottish mainland.

Much of Grampian is bleak, like tree-less Buchan, and the weather grim to contend with . . . especially for those pursuing the traditional industries of farming and fishing.

Now we have the oil industry — again a tough environment.

Yet the humour of the North-east belies its grim birth-place — and it's unique in Scotland.

It combines with salty language and its own expressive phrases to make a rich contribution to the wit of the nation.

And it has absorbed incomers over the years, easily adopting everyone from displaced persons and prisoners of war to oilmen into its culture.

The North-east knuckle's humour reflects the people — sometimes dour, mocking, blunt — and rarely gentle.

An accurate description of North-east folk was penned in a survey prepared for the 1963 Aberdeen meeting of the British Association for the Advancement of Science.

It said: "They are superficially somewhat grim, blunt, sardonic and non-commital, and yet beneath the surface, durable, self-reliant and sentimental in the better sense of the word."

While many of the stories collected here go back to the bygone days of the chaumer and nicky tams, the humour of the North-east has also kept up with the times . . . mocking, for example, the influx of Americans.

A farmworker is taking a haltered cow along a rural road when he is stopped by an American oilman.

"Say buddy, where are you taking that cow?"

"Ah'm takin her tae the bull."

"But surely, buddy, that's a job for the farmer."

"Na, na min — it's his tae be the bull."

Fittie fun!

Aberdeen's Fittie folk have long been known for their aloofness from the rest of the city, even in time of war regarding themselves as above the roles — ordinary and extraordinary — of their countrymen.

Hence the story that one night a rather odd character knocked on the door in the North Square at Footdee and asked for Mr Baxter.

"Aye, that's me" said the householder.

. Whereupon the stranger launched into: "The moon shines bright on the water tonight but the Rose of Tralee is not on the Dee she must be all at sea and the white foam screens the shores of foam."

The householder looked at his visitor for a minute and said: "Na na. It's nae me ye wint — it's Baxter the spy, he bides at Number 23."

*   *   *   *   *

A Fittie man advertised a pedigree Cairn terrier for sale and two prospective customers — one from Stonehaven and one from New Jersey — arrived at his door, together.

The Stonehaven man offered £15 and the American £20.

"Nah, I canna beat 'at", said the man from the Mearns: "£15 is my limit."

"Sold", said the man fae Fittie and off happily home went the Kincardineshire chiel.

As he left the American asked: "How come you sold the dog for £5 less than I was bidding?"

"Easy", said the Fittie fellow: "The dog can walk back to Aiberdeen, but it canna sweem the Atlantic."

Rusky business!

Regarding themselves as worldly — even sophisticated — men and women, North-easterners like to gently mock the still innocent.
This story illustrates the idea

A young farm lad was sitting in an old-style railway carriage when a striking girl entered. She had exceptionally full breasts straining tightly at her blouse and the young lad couldn't keep his eyes off them.

The girl became aware of his gaze and was slightly annoyed: "What are you staring at?"

"Och, ah'm sorry" said the young lad: "It's just that ah haven't seen anything like that since ah was at my mother's breast."

Slightly mollified the girl said: "Oh well, then . . ."

But the teenager still couldn't keep his eyes off her breasts and again the girl became aware of his gaze and told him off.

The young lad's discomfiture, however, couldn't dislodge his babyhood memories — or even mammaries — and he tried another tack.

"Look" he said: "I've got a tenner in ma pooch — ah'll gae it tae ye if ye would open your blouse and let me gie them a sook."

Well she was a practical girl and the carriage was empty and the £10 would come in handy.

So she agreed and unbuttoned her blouse allowing her large breasts to spill out for the young lad.

After only a minute or two the laddie's actions began to pleasurably affect the girl and thoughts of the full sex act overtook her.

"Would you", she whispered: "Like the ultimate?"

The lad raised his head from her nipples and said, wondering at his good fortune: "Dinna tell me ye've got a rusk in yer handbag?"

Just picture it!

Blackmail doesn't work very well with North-east folk.

A Buchan fairmer visiting London was in Soho approached by an attractive girl who promised him a very good time for £50.

The fairmer, having just sold "a lotta gran knowt at Maud" had the siller so he went with her to her flat.

In the middle of their encounter lights started flashing and the startled fairmer said: "Fit's at?"

The girl told him not to worry, that it was a lightning storm.

A week later back in Buchan the fairmer was hyowin' his neeps when a big limousine drove into the farmyard and a well-dressed man came out and approached him.

He was carrying an envelope and after saying he had come

from London produced some glossy photographs showing the fairmer in some startling positions with the girl — and both were naked.

The fairmer looked at the smart Londoner and said, "Weel, weel — they've cam oot fine."

"Yes", said the Londoner, "And I'm afraid they are going to cost you some money."

"Weel, weel — an did ye sae ye'd cam a' the wye fae London?"

"Yes."

"Weel, since ye've cam at far ah'll tak sax."

Ear, Ear!

There's the story of the canny man approached on Aberdeen docks by a girl who offers him "a good time" for £1.
"Is that richt?" he says, "Weel maybe — if ye hud ma lugs fin ye're daein it."
"That's okay" said the girl, well-used to the kinks of men.
After it was over — and she had complied with his request and been paid (but not tipped) her curiosity got the better of her.
"Why did you ask me to hold your ears while we were having a good time?" she asked.
"Weel", said the canny lad patiently, "Ye wis only asking a poun — an ah hid ah fiver in mah back pooch."

Rare breed!

A London society lady was touring North-east Scotland and was becoming annoyed with the varying accents and sometimes puzzling speech of her coach companions. So she turned to her neighbour and said haughtily: "In England we think breeding is everything."
"Och", said her Fraserburgh neighbour: "In the Broch we thinks it gweed fun an' a' — bit we files think o' ither things."

Speechless!

Overheard on a Torry bus:
"Hullo Maggie. Fit like?"
"Nae bad Beldie. This your quine?"
"Aye."
"Foo aul is she?"
"Twa."
"Gawa. Kin she spik?"
"Oh aye. Sae something tae the wifie, Sonia."
Child: "Awa an Shite."
"Oh, whatta rer spikker."

The cooncil hoose

An Aberdeenshire man — but a stranger to the city is being shown the sights by his friend.
They've looked at the theatre and Marischal College and as they dander doon Broad Street the countryman says: "Fit's 'at?"
"At's the Toon Hoose."
Whereupon the countryman falls down in a dead faint.
But after a few moments tended by his worried friend he revives and gets back onto his feet.
"Godalmichty — fit come ower ye — did ye hae a heart attack?"
"Na na — nae exactly — it's jist that ah've got ma name doon for ane o' them."

Lightly poached

Buchan poachers have a sense of logic bordering on the uncanny. On Ugie water near Longside a poacher was "catched" by a water bailiff.
"Ye canna fish here" said the bailiff: "This is Colonel Thamson's water."
"Ist? Weel weel fa's water is next tae this stretch?"
"Oh, up ere's Major Barclay's."
"Right ye are — ah,ll jist wite till it comes doon here and cast again."

Meanness is . . .

A man went into a wee Aberdeen shop and bought cigarettes and left without getting his change from a £10 note.
The shop-owner did try to attract the customer's attention ... by tapping the window vigorously — with a sponge.

Bully for gran!

The aul crafter wife suffers from deafness . . . at times
when it best suits her.
And when a new minister arrives at her kirk she sends her
teenage grand-daughter to his first service to tell her what
he's like.
On the girl's return she's immediately quizzed by the old
lady.
"Fit wis he like?"
"Nae bad — he spiks awfa loud."
"Eh — fit wis he like ah'm askin ye?"
"Ah'm teeling ye he his an awfa loud word."
"Eh — eh" said the old woman impatiently. "Ah'm askin
ye fit wis he like?"
And the girl loudly and angrily replied: "He bawls like a
bull!"
Instantly the aul crafter wife's eyes glinted with interest as
her ears caught the vital fact: "His he tho?"

Age no barrier!

*Age doesn't diminish the humour of a Nor'-easter, or whatever
else, let his optimism flag.*
*Witness the recent advertisement in the "Personal & Social"
column of the Aberdeen "Evening Express" —*

"Widower: Early 80s. House owner. Alone. Seeks
company, lady (65-75): possibly lasting friendship ..."

★   ★   ★   ★   ★

Snuffy and Babs

Two notorious Aberdeen ladies — Snuffy Ivy and her pal
Babs were in the Castlegate and short of money.
A country lad chances to pass them and Snuffy says:
"Widye, *sniff,* like a good time?"
"Aye", says the chiel: "Bit ah dinna ken if ah'm fit for
ye."

"Weel" says Snuffy scenting a conquest: "Ye can dae yer best."
"Ah dinna ken" says the country lad: "Ah'm sweer."
"Sweer, *sniff*", said Ivy:: "We can sort at, *sniff* — ye can hae baith o' us."
"Weel weel" said their target getting a little more interested: "Ah've nivver had twa weemin at the same time — foo much wid it cost?"
"Weel, *sniff*" said Snuffy cannily: "Foo muckle are ye willin tae pey?"
"Fit aboot a bob?"
"A bob, *sniff*" said Snuffy haughtily: "Fa dae ye think we are — the Tanner Sisters?"

Classroom Capers

An Aberdeen teacher asked her class of thirteen-year-old girls to write a short story.
And she advised tham that every story should contain a little religion, a bit of love, interest and mystery.
It was near class release time and one smart young girl returned with her story complete just one minute later.
It read: "My God, I'm pregnant. Who done it?"

✱   ✱   ✱   ✱   ✱

The same teacher elected two small boys to be in the school play.
Each had a brief walk-on speaking role.
The first had to say: "Oh fair maid I have come to snatch a kiss and fill your soul with hope."
The second boy on hearing this was to say: "Hark, I hear a pistol shot."

Night of the play came and the two boys were very, very nervous despite all.their rehearsals.
And the worst happened.
The first boy plunged on with: "Oh fair maid I have come to kiss your snatch and fill your hole with soap."
On hearing this the second boy even more nervous announced: "Hark I hear a shistal pot ... a postil shit ... er ... a pit shot ... a shit pot ... a cow shit ... bull shit ... oh bullocks, I didn't want to be in the bloody play in the first place."

Doctor, doctor . . .

A child-less North-east couple married for several years finally decide to see a doctor about their lack of fertility.
After examining each of them the doctor calls them back into his surgery.
And explains to the lady: "I'm afraid you have a condition called albuminuria."
"Fit's at?"
"It means there's a presence of albumen in your urine."
"Fit's at?"
"Albumen is the Latin for white of an egg."
Then the doctor turns to her husband and says: "I'm afraid you have a disaccharide in your blood."
"Fit's at?"
"It means a sugar — you have too much sugar in your blood."
"Dis 'at mean we canna mak bairns?"
"I'm afraid so — but there's some consolation for you both."
"Fit'a at?"
"I'm pleased to say you can make great meringues."

Stone me!

Three men in a railway carriage in Buchan are having a
dram and discussing their professions and worth.
First says: "I'm a doctor — I bring people into the world."
Second says: "I'm an undertaker — I bury them."
Third says: "I'm a stonemason — I pit a steen on the tap
o'them tae keep 'em doon."

Mind yir breeks!

*The record of emigrants from North-east Scotland who have
succeeded as soldiers, doctors, merchants and scholars is an
impressive one.*
*And there's great pride in the number of technical and
training colleges and other seats of learning as well as
Aberdeen University in the knuckle of Scotland.*
*But pride in their knowledge and a tendency to be "aff-takin"
shows in their humour about those who haven't education —
making them the butt of their jokes.*
*Topical these days is the artificial insemination of
women — but it's long been commonplace in the animal
world in the North-east.*
*And at the North-east marts this joke will always raise a
laugh.*

It concerns the crafter who had to go to market when the AI mannie was due.

"Noo", said the crafter tae his wife: "Fan the AI mannie comes tak him tae the byre, pint oot the coo, and be sure that he gets a basin a hate watter, an soap an a too'el an onything else he needs."

When the man from the AI arrived the crafter's wife did exactly as she was told, adding as she left the byre: "An there's a nail ahin the door far ye can hing yer breeks."

PUTT PUTT!

There's a marvellous story told in Buchan of the Peterhead golfer who died and sought entrance to paradise.

St Peter told him sternly that the heavenly rules were strict about admitting golfers — particularly those who swore.

"Ach weel, ah've only sworn aince" said the late golfer.

"Where was that?"

""Weel, ah wis playin' at Ballater and at the lang thirteenth ah hit ma drive inta a fun buss ..."

"Ah" said St Peter: "That's when you swore?"

"Na — ah took oot ma sivven iron and got it oot — bit it gaed intae a bunker."

"Ah" said St Peter: "That's when you swore?"

"Na — ah took oot ma san' wedge and blasted it oot bit it gaed richt across the green an ower the back inta a divot o' girse."

"Ah" said St Peter: "That's when you swore?"

"Na — ah took oot ma nine iron an skited it oot and it ran richt ower the hole and stopped ten feet past."

"Ah" said St Peter: "That's when you swore?"

"Na — ah jist calmly took oot ma putter, took ma time an' put it twa feet fae the hole."

"Ah" said St Peter: "That's when you swore?"

"Na — ah took ma putter again an' ..."

But St Peter interrupted: "Dinna tell me," he said, adopting a Buchan accent: "That ye misst the f.....' putt?"

PHRASES AND WORDS TO FLUMMOX

Good example is "Cha-in ma queed."

That's gibberish to folk outside the North-east knuckle of Scotland.

Maybe it's little wonder.

Literally translated the phrase means "Chewing the cud" — as the ruminating animals do.

And then, maybe, it has some meaning for those who have observed the quiet look of meditation that seems to overtake cows and sheep quietly and docilely "Cha-in the queed."

The late Ted Ingram, the innovative radio engineer who was more than 30 years with Aberdeen City Police, loved to tell this story relating to his native Strathbogie where his family had woollen mill connections.

In the 1920s farmers wanted their blankets made from the fleeces of their own sheep and not mixed with any other wool or substance.

So the conversation went:

Farmer: "Oo?"
Mill owner: "Aye, oo."
Farmer: "A' oo?"
Mill owner: "Aye, a' oo."
Farmer: "A' ae oo?"
Mill owner: "Aye, a' ae oo."

To explain (if it's necessary): *"oo"* (wool), *"aye"* (yes), *"a' "* (all), *"ae* (one).

"Aul farrant" is old-fashioned.
"Chauve" (struggle).
"Fair fleggit" (very scared).
"Farawa screed" (airmail or news from abroad).
"Fushionless" (powerless or lacking in energy).
"Girnal" (oatmeal chest).
"Gype" (stupid person).
"Nib" (nose).
"Snorl" (mix-up).
"Sotter" (mess).
"Stammagaster" (shock).
"Scunnert" (disgusted).
"Trauchled" (wearied or overworked).
"Vratch" (strictly translated 'wretch' but in North-east

Scotland more accurately describes a mischievous child.

(As a footnote to this section .... it's thought that as a **"partan"** is a crab there's a link between that and the North-east word **"crabbit"** (ill-tempered). For in some parts of Aberdeenshire and Kincardine bairns would be asked **'Fa ca'ad ye partan face?"** if they complained about things).

PHRASES TO FLUMMOX SOME
(A few in current use)

"The fat soo's airse is aye weel-creased."
(The rump of a portly pig is always well folded!).
"Ye wis fobbin like a fat kitlin."
(You were panting like a fat kitten.)
"See a bag o' ricky pig."
(Give me a bag of smoky bacon crisps.)
"A gurr in his bonnet."
(A slant to his cap that indicates ill-temper.)

PHRASES TO CONFUSE THE UNINITIATED

A Buchan farmer is telling an oilman that one of his prize cows from the dairy had her udder badly torn in an accident with a fun buss — but otherwise she was uninjured.

"Aw, that's too bad" said the oilman: "But how did a touring bus run into your cow and only damage her udder?"

"God almighty" said the farmer: "This was a fun buss at the corner o' the park."

Glossary note: A "fun buss" is a gorse bush or whin (hence'fun' — a thick, prickly shrub.

And that's an example of a phrase — and there are
many —that's in common use in Aberdeenshire but
completely unintelligible a few miles south of the city.
A word such as 'wun' is equally misconstrued.
'Wun' sounds like the first cardinal number . . . or the
recording of a victory.
And it's in the latter sense that North-east folk use it
wittily.
A drinking crony will say to another after a "fair night's
dram": "Did ye get hame aricht?" . . . "Aye, ah did at —
ah wun hame."

Writing on the wall . . . .

Sadly Aberdeen and the North-east now has as much paint-
spraying and mindless slogans on its public buildings as
any other area.
But in pubs in the city and country there are examples of
humour.
They may not have the accepted wit of comment scratched
on the walls of the ancient cities of Pompeii and Rome but
some have a little style.
For example:
    To Do Is To Be — Sartre
    To Be Is To Do — Rousseau
    Do Be Do Be Do — Sinatra.
Another at the bottom of a closet door in Ma Cameron's —
just above the four-inch gap from the floor — used to
caution the sitter: **"Beware of limbo dancers."**
And a one-liner in the urinal of the long-closed Bond Bar in
the Netherkirkgate accurately announced: **"Graffiti reading
causes wet feet."**
In a different setting — Aberdeen Sheriff Court has its
examples, perhaps not surprisingly on the Press benches

which double as jury seats during trials. One wonders
whether the jurors think the scribblings of bored reporters
have any merit.
Such as:
   "Life is a sexually transmitted disease."
   "A thing of beauty is a joy forever — until she runs off
with the milkman."
   "Sex is bad for one — but good for two." and
   "Say it with flowers — give her a Triffid."
And appropriately at Aberdeen airport:
   "The best things in life are duty-free."

That woman!

"I've just got my seventy-year-old mother-in-law a great job at £200 a week."
"At £200 a week — good God, what's the job?"
"A lollipop lady at Brands Hatch."

●●●●●●

"My mother-in-law has come to us for Christmas dinner for fourteen years ... this year I think I'll let her come in."

Phone sense ...

A sign in the Freelands Bar in Aberdeen's Castlegate was somewhat sobering.
It explained: "The publican is tired of relaying excuses when irate wives of late-night drinkers telephone to find out if they are in the bar.
Consequently the following telephone charges are now into effect, depending on replies as follows:
"Just left" — 25p
"On his way" — 50p
"Not here" — £1
"Fa?" — £2

page 19.........

Eh, fit?

Aberdonians have their own ideas about good manners — witness the deft touch from June Imray ....
describing a brief exchange betwen mother and son on a Torry bus.
Son: "Eh?"
Mother: "Dinna say eh — say Fit?"

Quick Ones ...

• *North-east Scots folk have a particular dislike of the letters 'W' and 'H' put together ... and the vowel 'E'. It's another form of their perversity or contermashiousness.*
Prominent examples are 'When' which becomes 'Fan', which handily makes the 'eeh' of the vowel into 'aah'! Similarly 'What' becomes 'Fat' ... and is often — as in Aberdeen and Banff and Buchan — reduced to 'Fit'.

• An oilman in Aberdeen asked the pretty young waitress if all Scots girls rolled their 'Rrs' as nicely as she did.
"Na na" she said: "It must be the sheen ah'm weerin."

• A big warehouse fire in Aberdeen had resulted in several brigade units from outside the city being summoned.
Hours later still fighting to quell the flames, a young fireman suddenly noticed a negro manning a hose beside him.
"Far are ye fae?" he asked.
"Africa" said the coloured man.
"Godalmichty," came the reply: "We jist cam fae Kintore."

Quickies . . .

• Two old Aberdeen men meet out on a stroll and one says: "I see Sandy Jamieson deid and left £10,000."
"Na, na — Sandy Jamieson niver left £10,000 — he was taen awa fae it."

• An Englishman, an Irishman and an Aberdonian were shipwrecked and found themselves floating in the storm-tossed Atlantic on a tiny raft.
The Englishman knelt down to pray, the Irishman knelt down to pray, and the Aberdonian threw himself overboard . . . he thought there was going to be a collection.

Mearns the Merrier!

The Mearns is weel-kent as a fertile part of the North-east — but there's another Mearns.
That's John — a man with a fertile imagination and a saying that for a few years was a catch-phrase in the area . . . **"Fit a gran' nicht we're haein"** — during his telecasts from Grampian TV.
Two short stories attributed to him.

It's mart day at Kittybrewster in 'is lad gets fou and a freen offers to rin him hame.
"Far dae ye bide again?"
"Echt" is the slurred reply.
Jist my luck on a coarse day thocht his pal but he got him in the car and through the teeming rain "wun his wye tae" Echt.
At the village outskirts he asked his drunken crony: "Far aboot in Echt?"
Came the shattering — still slurred — reply: "Echt Chapel Street!"

News at Keith!

The late Eddie Innes of Keith in Banffshire was a
correspondent in the fifties and sixties for many newspapers
— local and national.

While local journalists "kent Eddie fine" and how to enlist
his help, some high-powered executives in the south found
him sometimes a bit un-nerving.

But Eddie always did what he was asked — exactly as he
was asked.

And this rebounded on a news editor of the now-defunct
"Daily Sketch" of London.

For it happened that the Sketch learned of a good human story in Keith . . . that an irate cinemagoer had shot the projectionist of the local cinema because of a feeble film-showing.

The London news boss got hold of Eddie on the telephone and told him exactly what to do.

"You will go to the main police station in Keith, Mr Innes, and demand to see the most senior officer there.

"When you get an interview you will ask him about the callous shooting of a cinematic craftsman and you will ask him what happened.

"What's more, Mr Innes" said the hapless London-bound executive: "You will carefully and exactly note down every word of his reply — have you got that?"

"Ah certinly hiv" said Eddie, wondering why the man was so excited: "Ah'll phone ye back."

Fifteen minutes later Eddie was back on the phone to the "Daily Sketch" news editor in London.

"Is that you?" queried Eddie.

"Yes Mr Innes" said the great man impatiently: "Did you do what I asked exactly?"

"Ah did that" said Eddie: "Ah gaed tae the main police station in Keith.

"At wis easy — there's only ane ye see."

"Yes, yess" said the Londoner impatiently: "And did you get an exclusive interview with the senior officer?"

"Weel, ah suppose ah did, Ah jist gaed up tae the coonter and asked the serjent what had happened the day in Keith."

"Yes, yess" said the greatly excited top journalist, "And did you get down what he said?"

"Ah did that" said Eddie: "Ah hiv it here in ma note-book."

"Godalmighty" said the Englishman: "What did he say?"

And Eddie intoned on the telephone: "He said, 'Eddie there's aye something happening in Keith' " . . . and put down the receiver.

Pussy no more!

Seekers of love or sex in oil-boom Aberdeen resort to the local newspapers for opportunities — as apparent in the personal and social columns
And the ladies of the night have picked up some of the North-east's particular brand of wit and humour.
In the "Evening Express", for example:*"Part-time gentleman, 34-years plus required for social outings. No experience necessary as training will be given ..."*
Another Aberdeen quine asked in advertising: *"Would a tall well-built professional guy (28-35) like to spend some time brightening up the life of an affectionate young separated lady with own business and home."*
And yet another: *"Professional lady, 37, would like to meet gentleman to share life with and put some purpose back into it."*
Whether the lovelorn women got satisfactory replies is doubtful
For example, shortly after the start of the oil boom the London-based callgirls' union PUSSY — Prostitutes Union for Sexual Satisfaction Yourwye — sent emisssaries north to Aberdeen.
Despondently a PUSSY spokeswoman recorded after-wards: *"It was a waste of time .. . . there are too many willing amateurs in Aberdeen."*

★   ★   ★   ★   ★

Underlining the sense of humour that's prevalent in North-east newspaper columns — the "Huntly Express" used this comment on a successful sit-in at a factory hundreds of miles away in Scotland.
"Three cheers for the girls. They've managed to keep a factory going making jeans, in spite of all recesses, and now they're embarking on a new mystery product to give support to the women's front . . . it's a bra ca'd Abra."

The "Huntly Express" also carried this item: *"Fears of liquidation, erosion of productivity, splits in the grass roots, confusion in management, striking waves undermining continuity — and all at B.L. — British Leyland? No, Banff Links."*

*   *   *   *   *   *

Nun the wiser!

Two North-east nuns were waylaid on a dark Buchan road — by two irreverent but husky young men.
One nun began to murmur: "Father forgive them for they know not what they do."
But the other, native to the North-east, snapped, "Be quiet sister — this one does."

*　　*　　*　　*　　*　　*

No dummy!

A Buchan loon visiting London was drinking and dining in an expensive restaurant with some international farming friends.
At the coffee and brandy stage he stood up to go to the toilet and astonished everyone by asking for the bill.
Next day the Sun's heading read: **"Scot strangles English ventriloquist."**

Princely laughs . . .

The Royal family spend several months every year in the North-east of Scotland — with both Prince Charles and Prince Andrew choosing to spend parts of their honeymoon at Balmoral.
And it's obvious over the years that Charles picked up some of the humour that is so symbolic of the area.Not only in the comments he has made — but written.
For example the Royal author displayed considerable wit in his children's story — penned for his brothers Prince Andrew and Prince Edward — *"The Old Man of Lochnagar."*
This was published in 1980 — though written several years previously.

In it he refers to the old man's tiny friends . . . "little people who were called Gorms."

Then Prince Charles adds in brackets: *"That is why people in Scotland who don't have Gorms in their hills are called 'gormless'."*

Nae bad for a lad 'at spends only a few months in the Cairngorms — "bit he's neither feel nor gormless," as they say on Royal Deeside.

•When the Queen opened the St Fergus terminal in Aberdeenshire, the Press were much interested in a workhand called Beaton whose son saved Princess Anne from injury during the attempt on her life in London's Pall Mall.

He was then a Special Branch officer and the Princess's bodyguard.

And so at St Fergus the Queen was duly introduced to Mr Beaton, very much a North-east man.

When the crowd of journalists saw their chance they zoomed in on Mr Beaton and asked: *"What did the Queen say to you?"*

Mr Beaton said: *"Well, firstuva she spearet mi far ah bid."*

Of all the journalists round about only Jack Webster and this one had any idea what he was saying.

As Londoners, the radio and TV journalists thought grimly of lances, daggers or pikes, but two Buchan newsmen knew he meant that her Majesty had asked him where he lived!

• North-east people can readily see the opportunity for humour and wit in international situations.

And one was glibly translated with the widely-reported romance between Prince Andrew and actress Koo Stark.

It was certainly asked in one area of Buchan: *"If Andra tried his han' in Mustique an didna get onywye — dis 'at mean she's an attempted Koo?"*

(There's no answer to that!)

Holy wit!

There's a story of the minister going round his parish when he came on an old man pottering about in his beautiful garden "By jove" said the minister: "Together God and you are making a wonderful job of your garden."
"Maybe ye're richt" said the old man: "Bit ye shid ah seen't —fat a state it was in fan I took it ower fae God."

* * * * * *

The Holy Bible is a great literary work.
It's in the homes of the great majority of people in the "civilised" Western world.
It has been read and re-read.
Examined by scholars seeking answers, poetry, erotica, whatever . . .
They may have found the answers to questions about simplicity of verse, sex and morals, or whatever . . .
But they will not have found any humour in it.
For this basic ingredient in upbringing — particularly in the North-east of Scotland — is totally devoid of any sense of fun.
Mark Twain said: *"The secret source of humour is not joy, but sorrow . . . there is no humour in heaven."*
And maybe that's why J.C.Milne wrote:
"O Lord look doon on Buchan
And a' its fairmer chiels
For there's nae in a yer warld
Mair contermashious chiels."

The minister was lecturing a lusty farmworker who was known to be bedding more than just his wife. ·
"I didn't sleep with my wife before I was married", he said: "Surely you didn't either?"
"Ah dinna ken 'an", he paused, "Fit wis 'er maiden name?"

Simple logic . . .

The harsh and unpredictable weather of Banffshire and Buchan has produced many memorable comments from a long-suffering people.
A clear day in Cullen brought a question from a tourist to a local as he peered across the Moray Firth at dimly distant hills.
"Is that Inverness-shire across there?"
And the reply: "Aye, fin ye can see that it's ga'in tae rain.
"Fin ye dinna — it is raining."

*   *   *   *

Grouses . . .

Jokes, stories and comments about whisky are naturally plentiful.
Offered a dram — the pitiful sixth of a gill measure used in Aberdeen — a man asked his friend: "What's this?"
"It's a malt — twelve years old."
"Weel my God, it hisna grown much."

*   *   *   *

A ghillie on the Dee had an American out for a day's salmon fishing on a dreich wet day.
Though conditions were good the American was unlucky and never got a nibble.
But he consoled himself with the contents of a hip-flask yet . . . never offered the ghillie a dram.
Then he took out his pipe and tried to light it in the drizzle with a match
"Goddamit Jock — isn't there anything dry I can strike my match on?"
Said the ghillie: "Ye micht try ma throat."

Cross talk!

Long-suffering taxi drivers in Aberdeen have their own
inbuilt sense of humour to keep them going.
It was brought home to a visitor who hired a cab in the
city centre.
At traffic lights the driver failed to move though they
were at green — because an old lady was still crossing.
However this did not stop the driver of a car behind
becoming annoyed and hooting his horn.
The taxi driver kept calm and quietly got out of the car
and approached the irate driver.
The cabman pointed to his own vacant seat and told the
angry driver: *"You get in and drive over her — I haven't got
the heart."*

* * * * * * * * * * * * * *

A smooth-talking Englishman called on the humble but
finely-furnished home of an old lady on Deeside looking for
antiques.
"Ah've naethin' like 'at" she said.
And despite his persuasive manner she would not allow him
into her home to look around.
But he did spot an ornately-carved wooden box in her lobby
— which he instantly recognised as being of considerable
value.
"I'll give you £400 for that old box" he said hoping to
financially edge his way into the house.
"Na na" said the old dear, gently but firmly closing the door
on him: "Ah widnae hae onywye to keep ma sticks."

Pregnant pause!

Some Buchan farmers have a knack of putting an awkward
situation into perspective . . . to suit their own viewpoint.
At Maud mart one sale day two farmers were standing at
the ringside watching the stirks being sold.
One of them — eyes still fixed on the beasts — said out
of the blue: "That's an awfa thing your loon's daen tae my
quine."
There was a pause then the reply: "Fit's that like?"
Another pause: "He's gaen an bairnt her."
Yet another pause and then: "Dam't he's a careless
bugger 'at — last wike he broke a grape."

Father, dear father!

*Humour starts young — perhaps unwittingly — in the
classrooms of Aberdeen.*
A ten-year old was aware of a marital split in his home
which had given him a "new" father.
And he told his teacher: "I'm like one of my das — but nae
like the ither."
And the same boy told his chum he wouldn't be able to see
him on Saturday afternoon bacause: "In the morning I'm
ga'in oot wi' mah first da an' then in the aifterneen I'm ga'in
oot wi' mah second da."

* * * * * * * * * * *

Just the ticket!

There's humour in everything for Aberdonians as well.
In October, 1982, the Queen Mother visited the Central Library
in Aberdeen — a modest event of which everyone was not
aware.
And so in a Mastrick pub one drinker was overheard to say to

his friend: "Ye winna guess fa ah sa at the library — the Queen Mother."
"Ah didna ken she was a member there," came the reply.

Class of their own!

The late James Scotland was adroit at using North-east humour to take the pompousness out of ceremony.
An example was his address as Prinicpal of Aberdeen College of Education to the 1983 summer graduates which he peppered with jokes.
"We have steadily drifted away from formality. Ceremonial occasions, occasions like this, have gone out of fashion.
"The day will come, doubtless, when they will vanish altogether.
"I can only say, with the old lady in mind who was told that the End of the World was nigh, 'Ah weel, thank God it's lasted my time'."
It was Mr Scotland's farewell address after 36 years in Scotish education but there was nothing sad about it.
With glee he told of the eight-year-old boy who was asked how the Israelites got across the Red Sea and replied: "Fine."
Went on to tell of the 14-year-old who when asked to identify Archbishop Makarios of Cyprus answered: "He is a man we were asked about in a test."
Praising the students for their industry and application he recalled the Primary 5 pupil who was asked by the Inspector: "Have you had to work out ALL these examples of the same sum?"
And chuckled as he gave the boy's answer: "Aye, hellish, intit?"
Himself a distinguished dramatist Mr Scotland included in that address a masterly Nativity Play that was the work of a ten-year-old author.

Joseph: "I hear Herod's going to kill all the boy babies."
Mary: "Tch, if it's not one thing it's anither! Fit'll we dae?"
Joseph: "Fit aboot fleein'?"
Mary: "Good idea. Far till?"
Joseph: "Fit aboot Egypt?"
Mary: "OK — You get the donkey and ah'll get Jesus."

Fast laughs!

• A Buchan fairmer was stopped by a shapely black girl near the old Stanley Hotel on Aberdeen's quayside.
"Would you like to take me home?" she asked provocatively.
"Fit? A' the wye tae Africa?"

●●●●●●●●●●●●●●

• *A coachload of New Pitsligo tourists is turning into Little Belmont Street and the guide says: "We're now passing Ma Cameron's — one of the oldest inns in Aberdeen."*
Voice from the rear of the bus: "Fit wye?"

●●●●●●●●●●●●●●

• A barber's shop in Ellon is now situated in a former public toilet . . . and the owner's name is Alan.
With typical North-east humour the salon is called: "Ur in Al's."

Mean — wha, us?

Meanness has long been the joke prerogative of the Aberdonian. It's something he relishes and he has happily laughed at his own apparent discomfiture for decades in the music hall . . . even on postcards.
We've all seen a picture of Aberdeen's Union Street

absolutely deserted with the caption: *"Aberdeen on a street flag day"* and the same packed street with: *"Aberdeen on a house-to-house collection day."* And heard sayings like . . . *"During the cold winter months Aberdeen housewives always wash the dishes last thing at night . . . so that they can use the water for their hot water bottles."*

Or the advertisement in a shop window in Aberdeen — *"Bring your golf ball here to be re-covered."*

Or the story of the canny Aberdonian who came home unexpectedly and caught his wife in the arms of a neighbour.

He grabbed his single-barrel shotgun and shouted: *"Stand behind your lover you faithless bitch — I'm going to shoot you both."*

There's only one real competitor to Aberdeen for the 'meanest city' tag —the unlikely town of Gabrovo in Bulgaria.

In fact a few years ago there was a contest in Aberdeen to find the "meanest' joke between the two towns.

One of the best — or worst — that the Gabrovians could muster was that they cut the tails off their cats in winter so that less heat will escape when they enter or leave.

But the Aberdeen counter was neater. Traditionally Aberdonians don't paint or paper their walls — it would decrease the size of the rooms.

A wry twist . . .

"Fit's afore ye will nae gyang bye ye."
Even the gloomy subject of death takes a wry twist in Buchan humour.

An example is the habit in the area of locating kirks in the centre of parishes — where there are rarely houses and the living. And those that are nearby — *"the nearest tae kirk, the furthest fae grace"* — don't darken its doors in an upright condition.

Rathven, near Fraserburgh is an appropriate case . . .
giving rise to the sardonic couplet:
"The road tae the kirk o' Rivven
"Far gangs mair deid than livvin."

* * * * * *

A worried wife!

An old crofter is on his death bed being comforted by his wife
and her sister.
He turns to his wife and says: "We've had a gran' life thegither
but somethin's aye bothered me for years.
"Jock an' Jimmy were twa gran' strappin' loons an are noo fine
men — bit Sanny his aye been a shargar.
"Tell minoo — is he my sin?"
And his wife replies: "Oh aye, ah'll sweer tillt."
At that the crofter dies a happy man and a while later the
widow's sister says: "At wis a funny thing Mac asked ye before
he deid."
"Ah ken at" says the widow: "I wis worried for a meenit — ah
thocht he wis gyan tae ask aboot the ither twa."

* * * * * *
Road sense . . .

North-east drivers are notoriously bad — bringing down
upon themselves the wrath of the more expert used to
motorways, lane discipline and "keepin' tae yer ain side
o' the road."
One old farmer heedlessly sticking to the middle of the
road was being constantly exhorted by his front-seat
passenger to watch "yer side o' the road."
Finally, tired of his warnings, the old farmer turned to
his passenger and said: "Will ye shut up min — ye'll see
the ither side o' the road fin we're ga'in hame."

All at sea . . .

Two farmers on their first sea cruise found themselves a bit out of their depth when the wind and weather took a turn for the worse.

But one of them had a bit of landlubberly philosophy to understate the situation:

"Aye," he said surveying the huge waves: "She's a bit roch, Jimmy — she could dae wi' a good strake o' the harraas."

Golf wit . . .

There's a terse touch of North-east humour in the story told about the late golfing character of Aberdeen, 'Chapper' Thomson. Chapper was taking the names of entrants to a tournament at the Links and most were just giving surnames and initials. As another competitor arrived Chapper, without looking up, asked "Name?"

Which drew the reply: "Major D Graham."

Again without looking up Chapper remarked: "We're here to play golf — nae sodgers."

(The same Major Graham in fact succeeded Chapper as Secretary of the North East Golf Alliance.)

Wise sayings . . .

Among its share of couthy proverbs the North-east has couched in its own language the following examples all wonderfully self-explanatory:

- "Canna dee sits at the back o' winna dee's door."
- "Dae naethin' in the day that'll gar ye greet at nicht."
- "Gin ye hidna been amang the craws ye widna hae been shot."
- "It's nae fit ye hae bit fit ye dae wi' fit ye hae that coonts."
- "The tink and the toff's a' the same tae me."

Fishermen's tales . . .

North-east fishermen have their own derisory and localised sense of humour.

In the days when Cruden Bay — or more correctly the Port Errol part of it — was a thriving wee harbour port the local fishermen were the butt of jokes by men from other airts.

And a Cruden Bay man would rise angrily when baited with the word 'Waversooth.'

This harks back to the days when the Cruden Bay folk were said to lure boats in bad weather onto the rocks, the Skare's o' Cruden, south of the harbour.

When they started to edge into the safety of the harbour the Cruden Bay folk would wave their lanterns apparently warning them to go further south before turning to starboard.

And so 'Waversooth' became a derogatory term for a Cruden Bay fisherman.

Similarly you could guarantee anger by saying to a Boddamer — a fisherman from Boddam — "Fa hung the monkey?"

This is derived from the old rhyme:

"There was a boat gid roon the coast.
"An a' the crew of her were lost —
"Except the monkey at the post.
"An the Boddamers hung the monkey-o."

Again it's said that Boddam fisherfolk lured boats onto the rocks in foul weather so that they became wrecks — and in their eyes could be plundered.

But only if all souls were lost — and the "Monkey" story ridicules the lengths that some would go to share in the booty.

And there's added barbed wit in the suggestion that it wasn't a monkey that the Boddamers hung, anyway — but a hapless, coloured East-Indian seaman, traditionally employed on European freighters — the Lascar.

To this day bitter comments are kept up by rival North-east ports.

For example a Peterhead fisherman telling a story always makes sure that it's someone from another port that is the butt.

So they ask you: "Did you hear the story of the Buckie man ..."

A mild instance is the case of the Buckie boat that got its nets entangled with those of a Kirkcaldy vessel while fishing in the 'Sooth Firth' — the Firth of Forth and strange waters to the Buckie man.

And in the shouting match that followed it's the Buckie man — according to Peterhead fishermen — who is 'credited' with yelling: "Jist ye wite till ye cam tae Scotland an we'll sort ye oot."

Laughter in court!

Even a sheriff can find humour in cases brought before the courts of North-east Scotland.

In Aberdeen an oilman acccused of sending blue movies out to the North Sea had readily admitted his involvement . . . but not his desire to corrupt.

He had offered to pay a fine to the Customs and Excisemen who brought the charge.

But they were determined that he be brought to justice for his efforts to corrupt the womanless wilderness of the North Sea.

So the man was brought to court and under the persistent questioning of a deputy procurator fiscal agreed he had sent out the soft porn films.

He also admitted he had told them he had another movie at home and they accompanied him to his door where the oilman told his wife: "They've come about the blue movie — could you get it?"

The fiscal than explained to Sheriff Roy Stewart of Elgin:
"The accused's wife came down the stairs with a Finefare
carrier bag containing the film."
"With what?" said the Sheriff: "A Finefare carrier bag — I
didn't know their range extended that far."

Jailhouse humour!

The range of humour produced in the North-east is wide
and it survives in the toughest, grimmest surroundings . . .
like Peterhead Prison.

In a brilliant, witty address jail Governor Alf Smith had
delegates to the 1982 Scottish Prison Officers' Association
conference in stitches with his description of life inside and
outside the jail.

Even escape attempts, rooftop demonstrations and riots
were humorously dealt with by Mr Smith.

"We have a fine inmates harriers club" he told delegates:
"Which indulges in spasmodic but frenetic activity and
which gives all of us the opportunity of being associated
with all that's best in amateur athletics.

"We have had occasional meetings of the 'do-it-yourself'
class which is remarkable because of its interest in the re-
arrangement of high-level architecture.

"This we have found stimulating but sometimes puzzling
because the members of this class prefer to act in ad hoc
fashion without consultation and without first discussing
their plans with management.

"Even when friendly advice is given by management there
is a reluctance by the class to concede that their
architectural alterations lack grace and style."

Mr Smith told the delegates that another feature of 1981 at
Peterhead had been "the way in which we have all had to
take a renewed interest in hygiene with some of your

colleagues —not willingly — being exposed to new
methods of waste disposal, and which are not traditional."
Not much has changed for the better in the jail in the years
since.

* * * * * *

On a bleak, windy and wet Aberdeen day an American
oilman already subjected to flight delays is annoyed when
stopped for a Customs baggage check.
"Godawlmighty — I've been all over the goddam world
and this must be the ass-hole of it."
"Aye, aye, maybe so" said the Customs officer cannily:
"An I suppose ye'll be passin' through."

Arise my Sun!

The following is not native to the North-east in origin but must
be one of the most photo-copied items in the area, so proud of
its weekly, provincial daily and evening, and national newspaper
presence.

*"The Times" is read by the people who run the country, the
"Daily Mirror" is read by the people who think they run the
country, the "Guardian" is read by the people who think they
ought to run the country, the "Morning Star" is read by the
people who think the country ought to be run by another
country, the "Daily Mail" is read by the wives of the people who
run the country, the "Daily Express" is read by the people who
think the country ought to be run the way it used to be run, the
"Daily Telegraph" is read by the people who think it still is and
the "Sun" is read by people who don't care who runs the
country as long as they've got big tits.*

• • • • • •

The Pub Crawl . . .

Thirty-three pubs are mentioned in W.J.Buchan's well known
"The Pub Crawl" as well as the old Tivoli Theatre.
Nine are gone forever but there are plenty replacements.
However, producing "The Pub Crawl" with the names of bygones
will bring out wistful memories among older drinkers.
And the humour expressed by Mr Buchan is typical of the
Aberdonian.

"THE PUB CRAWL" by W.J.Buchan

There's plenty pubs in Aberdeen
Frae Torry ower t'Mastrick
And I have been in maist o' them
My stomach's something gastric.

'The White Cockade' — nae lemonade
And 'Gleggie's famous Cellar'
To 'The Grampian Bar' — and that's nae far
I've drank wi' mony a feller.

'The Waterloo' — where I've been fu'
The 'Neptune' doon in Fittie
And 'Simon's Bar' whar mony a tar

Goes lookin' for a bittie.
The 'Empire', 'Club', and 'Bon-Accord'
And of course — 'The Tartan Divie'
For mony a rare nicht I've spent there
Along wi' Snuffy Ivy.
There's 'Paterson's' — 'The Waverley'
Aye — even in the 'Tiv'
Wi' half a dollar in my pooch
An' dressed up like a spiv!
A nip an' a pint in 'The Union Bar'
An export in 'The Lorne'
A strong ale in the good old 'Crit'
Forget aboot the morn!
I've struggled in 'The Hop Inn'
Survived in 'The Royal Oak'
That's a helluva place tae ha'e a glaiss

It's nae for gentle folk!
I've dragged my feet up Union Street
And nipped in tae 'The Grill'
A glaiss o' rum an' a packet o' crisps
Oh I like t' ta'e my fill!
'The Star and Garter's jist roon by
'The Palace Bar' as weel
I've stood there aye till closin' time
An' staggered oot fair feel!

'The Frigate' for a pint o' stout
'The Henhoose' for a laugh
'The Wallace' for a game o' darts
An' a pint o' half an' half!
'The Coach and Horses' — Friday nicht
Or upstairs in 'The Swan'
I like a bit o' sing-song

Tae wash doon my Black an' Tan!
There's 'Allan's Bar' in George Street
Sit doon tae pie and peas
'The Balaclava's my next stop
I'm nearly on my knees!
Then 'Winter's Bar' — 'The Northern'
And ower tae 'The Crag'
'Twas there I nearly foonered
As I shoved awa a bag!
But onward to the 'Butcher's Arms'
There's nothing like a crawl
For booze is jist the very thing
T'keep awa the cauld!
'The Stag's Head's roon in Hutcheon Street
Last stop afore the club
I've nae much cash — I'll ha'e a slash
A handy thing — a pub!
Well here I am at hame again

Now whar the hell's my key?
The wife — she's waitin' wi' the boot
Tae hear my latest lee!
Wi' the thockt o' a' this wallop an' wine
I'm feelin' kind of merry
So I'll awa — but mind the morn
I'll see you in 'The Hairy'.

"Ye Olde Frigate Bar" gets an honourable mention in another few verses penned by an English exile who spent most of her Hogmanay trying to sample some of the 120 blends and malts stocked by the owner Derek North.

HOGMANAY 1974 (To the tune of Barnyards of Delgaty)

We traivelled up to Aberdeen
Tae see the last o' sivventy four,
We spent oor time at the Frigate Bar
There's a real fine welcome at the door.
CHORUS: Nips of whisky, halves of heavy,
        Have a game of domino,
        Far's yer glass, I see it's empty,
        Hae a dram afore ye go.
The weather it wis affa fine,
Sunshine, blue sky, nae a cloud,
Walk to town, work up a thirst,
Ging in and see the usual crowd.
CHORUS
First a Bells and then a Dewars
Auchentoshan's on the shelf,
Fiddich, Dronach, Glen Morangie,
Take yer pick and suit yerself.
CHORUS
Noo some can drink in the Prince of Wales,
And some can drink in the Cavalier,

But half seas over in the Frigate Bar
Is the way tae say a 'Guid New Year.'
CHORUS
So here's to Derek and his cronies,
They'll welcome you when you arrive,
Jist hae one of the hundred and twenty,
A' the best for seventy-five.
CHORUS

D.M.A. 6.1.75

Overheard at the bar . . .

• The trouble with oral sex is that just talking about it is no substitute for the real thing. *(Gray's Inn)*

• He's nae mean — he's jist got an impediment in his reach. *(Frigate)*

• The meek may inherit the earth but they dinna get the mineral rights. *(Kippie Lodge)*

• You've made a happy man feel very old.

(The Happy Valley)

* * * * * *

Off the rails!

At one of the old manually-operated railway level crossing gates the linesman started to close the gates over the road.

He had only one of the twin gates pulled over when the telephone in his signal box began to ring.

The signalman left one gate open after checking his watch to make sure there was time and left to answer the telephone.

A minute later on his return he found an irate English motorist hopping up and down.

"My good man" he exclaimed: "Why the devil did you leave the gates half shut?"

"Weel" said the old railwayman: "Ah wis half-expectin' a train."

Young American oilman gets on the train at Aberdeen and finds every seat taken except one on which is seated a small lap dog belonging to a large middle-aged lady.

"Excuse me, ma'am" he says politely: "Would you mind moving your little dog?"

He is totally ignored by the woman, not just once but three times she snootily disregards him.

That's too much for the American who suddenly opens the carriage window and throws the hapless dog outside.

There are a few seconds of stunned silence then an Aberdonian sitting opposite says: "Ken 'is, you Yanks is funny.

"Ye drive on the wrang side o' the road, ye ate wi' yer fork in the wrang han' — and noo ye've thrown the wrang bitch oot the winda."

The Chaumer . . .

*Lots of things were talked about — and done — in the
chaumer.*
*And very often there was a mixture of men from callow youth
to oldtimer bothied together.*
*In such a chaumer were three lads — two young men and a
veteran "O shalt an shim."*

One night one of the lusty lads announced: "Ah think
ah'll awa and see Helen up-the-glen."
Helen was a bonny quine and readily available and his
friends knew what he was after.
And within an hour he was back.
"Weel, fit like did ye get on?" asked his young chaumer
friend.
"Jist gran'," said the smirking loon, "What a passion she
has."
This fired the other young lad and he announced: "Ah
think ah'll awa an see Helen an' a' " — and off he went.
Within the hour he was back — smirking.
"Weel, fit like did ye get on?"
"Jist gran'," said his pal: "What a passion she has."
"Weel weel, now" said the old man of the trio: "Maybe
ah shid ging an' see Helen masel' ".
"Weel" said the young men doubtfully: "If ye think ye
can manage 'er — she's an awfa passion."
But the old man went off up the glen and the young lads
got a little worried as the evening passed and he'd never
returned.
"Maybe she's been ower much for him", said one
worriedly.
"Ach, jist keep a calm sooch" said the other: "We'll wite
an' see."
And so it was next morning before the old man
wandered with glazed eyes back to the chaumer.

"Weel, weel" said the young men, "Helen's fairly full o'
passion, isn't she, eh? eh? — what a passion eh?"
The old man looked at them and said: "Aye, she his at
— and what a patience, what a patience!"

Flower power!

Many of the towns of North-east Scotland have their own
newspapers — and they continue to flourish with a style that
the modern tabloids sometimes envy.
Take the imagination behind a headline in the "Banffshire
Journal" about a common and garden event:
**"Action packed programme lined up for Aberchirder
Flower Show."**

A fair cop!

*Police officers are rarely attributed with a sense of wit or
humour but in the Grampian force they try.*
*Here are two examples of their "Thoughts for the Month" from
their accident and safety bulletins.*

- "The road to happiness has a lot of parking spaces."
- "Those drivers who have been caught out by slippery
roads are easy to spot. They are sitting bolt upright behind the
wheel, their knuckles are white and they have a surprised
look on their faces . . ."

Even the youngest police officers try to give the impression that
they are in complete control of the situation. That includes a
worldy approach to their own colleagues.
And a young PC — the late, lamented Bill Kinnaird — fell foul of
that one night while front-seat passenger in a patrol car when
the radio-telephone buzzed.
Young Bill (as he was then) snatched it up and listened
carefully.
Then he slammed it down and said to the Sergeant driving: "It's
the code."

"Fit bloody code?"
"You ken, you ken — the code."
"Fit bloody code?"
"You ken — the code 4234340."
"Ah dinna ken ony bloody code — we're near Queen Street we'll ask the controller."
Back at HQ the Sergeant says to the controller: "Fit's this, fit's this aboot a bloody code?"
"Ah dinna ken onything aboot a bloody code — fit bloody code is this?"
"Tell him" says the Sergeant to the hapless Young Bill.
"It's the code 4234340" he replied.
"At's nae a bloody code" says the controller: "That was 'Go to 34 Seaforth Road'."
(Bill swore to me that was true.)

Bird in the hand . . .

About 25 years ago Grampian TV ran a series of "Bothy Ballad Nichts" that led to an upsurge in the.popularity of cornkister music and chaumer-style comedy.
One of the successful groups was the Kingseat Bothy Billies led by Donald McBeath who was a member of staff at the hospital.
This is one of Donald's jokes:

Two patients are strolling through the grounds of Kingseat when one is unfortunately hit on the head.by seagull shot.
"Godalmichty" he says to his pal: "Hive ye got a bit o' paper on ye?"
His friend looks sadly up at the seagull soaring above them and says: "Och, never mind 'at — ye'll nivver catch it noo."

KGB in North-east!

Grampian Regional Councillor Paul Miller is well-known for his constant remarks about the KGB.
This has nothing to do with the Russian Secret Police — just his knack of getting more publicity for the campaign of which he is chairman: "Keep Grampian Beautiful."

* * * * * * * * * *

Chinese Cracker!

Top North-east newsman Arthur Binnie is credited with a humorous one-liner during a journalists' facility visit to the far east.
When Arthur and his colleagues finally got past the suspicious Red Guards to a vantage point on the 'Great Wall' Arthur threw out his arms and shouted: "Hullawerr China!"

Is the manager in?

Alex Salmond, the SNP MP for Banff and Buchan, may be one of the incomers to the North-east but he won a round of applause — and probably quite a few votes — when he told this typical North-east story like a native to a distinguished audience in Peterhead of the 1988 Scotish Prison Officers' Association conference delegates.

It concerned, said Mr Salmond, the Turriff farmer who went to his far from friendly bank and asked: "Kin I see the manager?"
To be told by an assistant: "I'm sorry, the manager has died very suddenly — it's a great shock to us all."
"Weel weel," said the farmer, shook his head and left.
But next day back he came and again asked to see the manager.
The assistant was troubled: " I told you yesterday that the

manager had died suddenly" he repeated: "It was a great
shock to us all — we are all grief stricken."
"Weel weel," said the farmer, and left as before.
But back he came the next day with the same inquiry
and the next and of course always got the same reply
from the perplexed assistant.
On the fifth day when he asked yet again to see the
manager the assistant's veneer of patience cracked.
"Look you cretin," he yelled: "You dunderheid. The
manager has passed away, he has departed this earth, he
has joined his forefathers, he has gone to the great
banking hall in the sky.
"Don't you understand? Are you deaf?
"THE MANAGER IS BLOODY DEAD!"
"Oh aye, I unnerstan',"said the farmer: "I heard ye the
first time . . . I jist like to hear ye say it."

page 47........

Last one . . .

The late North-east journalist Jimmy Gillespie was very
impressed with the still handsome old spinster he was
interviewing in the remote hamlet of Gallowhill, near
Tomintoul.
She was the subject of a report by the Registrar General
for Scotland about population figures — and had been
singled out by the Daily Record as being the one person
then living in the once thriving wee Banffshire village.
Interview concluded Jimmy gently asked: "Why is it that
such a fine-looking woman like you is still unmarried?"
To which came the reply: "I was waiting for a lum hat —
and a' the bunnets passed me by!"